D1616480

# C U T A W A Y

# DIGGERS

## AND OTHER

## CONSTRUCTION MACHINES

## JON RICHARDS

COPPER BEECH BOOKS

BROOKFIELD, CONNECTICUT

© Aladdin Books Ltd 1999

Designed and
produced by
Aladdin Books Ltd
28 Percy Street
London W1P 0LD

First published in
the United States in 1999 by
Copper Beech Books,
an imprint of
The Millbrook Press
2 Old New Milford Road
Brookfield, Connecticut 06804

Editor
Michael Flaherty

Consultant
Steve Allman
Design
David West
Children's Book Design
Designer
Simon Morse
Illustrators
Simon Tegg & Ross Watton
Picture Research
Brooks Krikler Research

All rights reserved
Printed in Belgium

Library of Congress
Cataloging-in-Publication Data
Richards, Jon, 1970-
Diggers and other construction machines /
by Jon Richards ; illustrated by Simon
Tegg.
p.   cm. — (Cutaway)
Includes index.
Summary: Text and cross-section
illustrations present the design and uses of
various digging and excavatng machines,
including the backhoe loader, walking
drag-line excavator, and mining shovel.
ISBN 0-7613-0905-5 (lib. bdg.). —
ISBN 0-7613-0790-7 (trade)
1. Excavating machinery—Juvenile
literature.  [1. Excavating machinery.
2. Machinery.]  I. Tegg, Simon, ill.  II. Title.
III. Series.
TA732.R53   1999          98-51882
624.1'52—dc21          CIP  AC

5 4 3 2 1

# CONTENTS

# INTRODUCTION

Construction machines can be found wherever any building work is being done, from putting up small houses to laying long roads. Over the years, these mighty machines have replaced the work of hundreds of people. Today, enormous shovels can gouge huge holes in the ground, boring machines can dig long tunnels deep underground, and excavators can pull down tall buildings.

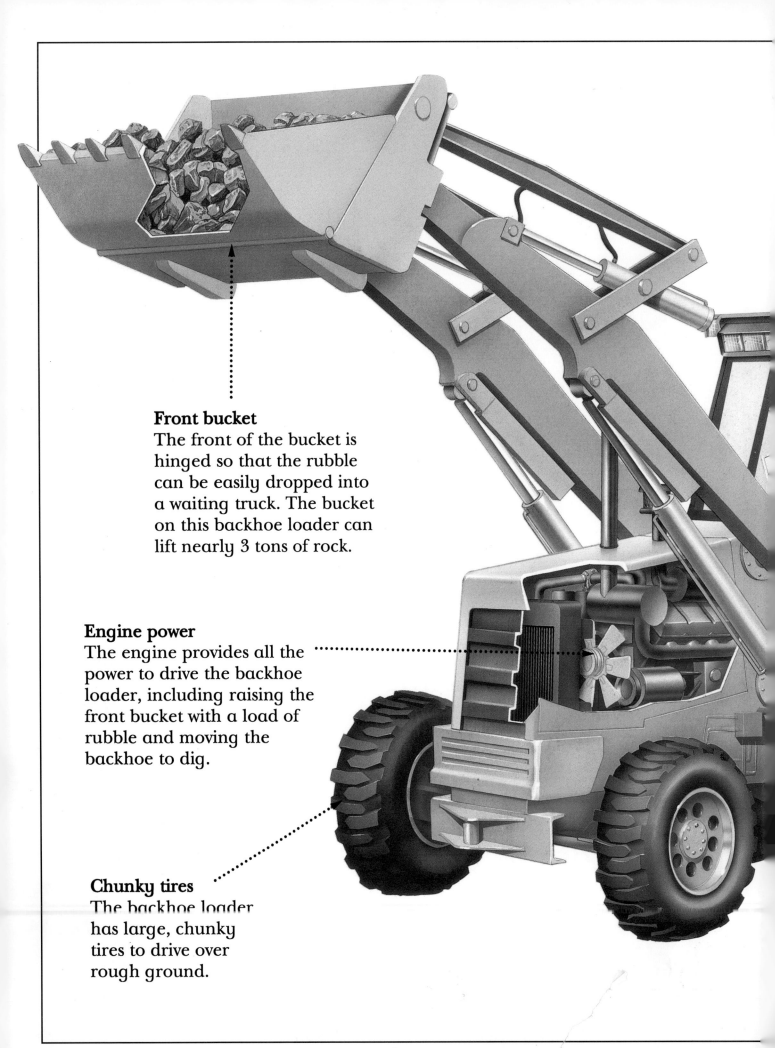

**Front bucket**
The front of the bucket is hinged so that the rubble can be easily dropped into a waiting truck. The bucket on this backhoe loader can lift nearly 3 tons of rock.

**Engine power**
The engine provides all the power to drive the backhoe loader, including raising the front bucket with a load of rubble and moving the backhoe to dig.

**Chunky tires**
The backhoe loader has large, chunky tires to drive over rough ground.

**Backhoe**

At full stretch, the backhoe can reach out, or down, as far as the height of three adults lying head to toe. It is moved by controls at the back of the driver's cab.

**Stabilizers**

These special arms reach out to take the weight off the back wheels and to provide a steady platform when the backhoe is being used.

# BACKHOE LOADER

This unusual-looking machine is possibly the most useful digger on any building site. It has tools fitted to its front and to its back. On the front is a huge scoop, or bucket, that can be used to scoop up rubble. On the back is a movable arm, called a backhoe. This can be used to dig trenches or pull down buildings. It can also be fitted with different tools to do other jobs, such as a pneumatic drill (*see* page 18) and a mechanical claw.

5

# Diggers can come in

## Foundation piles

When a tall building is being put up, it needs very deep foundations so it won't sink into the ground. Special cranes fitted with huge drill bits (*below*) dig holes into which the foundation piles are sunk.

## Dredger

Not all diggers are used on land. A dredger (*above*) digs up mud from the bottom of the sea or a river. This stops the waterway from getting blocked.

# all shapes and sizes.

## Skid steer

This tiny building machine (*below*) is called a skid steer. It is very useful in small spaces because it can turn very tight corners.

## Mini excavator

A mini excavator (*left*) is used where space is tight. With its small arm and bucket, it can dig very narrow trenches. The body of the excavator above the tracks can rotate in a full circle.

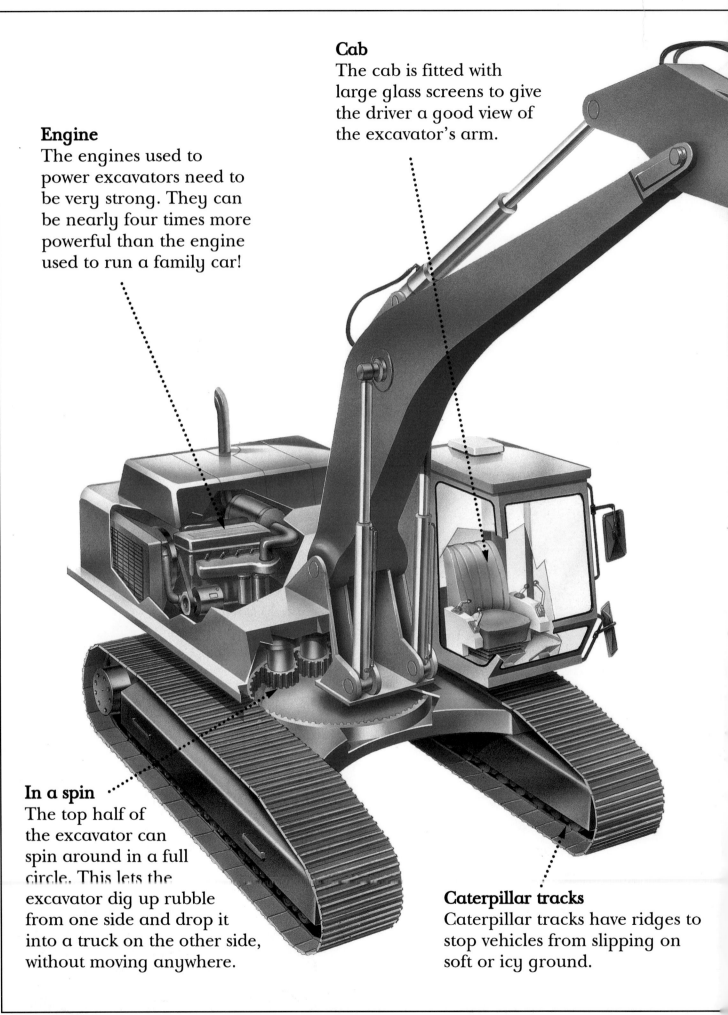

**Engine**
The engines used to power excavators need to be very strong. They can be nearly four times more powerful than the engine used to run a family car!

**Cab**
The cab is fitted with large glass screens to give the driver a good view of the excavator's arm.

**In a spin**
The top half of the excavator can spin around in a full circle. This lets the excavator dig up rubble from one side and drop it into a truck on the other side, without moving anywhere.

**Caterpillar tracks**
Caterpillar tracks have ridges to stop vehicles from slipping on soft or icy ground.

## Hydraulic arm

The engine pumps fluids in and out of hydraulic rams on the excavator's arm. Inside these rams, the fluids push pistons in and out, moving the arm.

## Hinged bucket

The bucket on an excavator is hinged, allowing it to be moved up and down, like your wrist.

## Sharp teeth

As the arm pulls the bucket back, sharp metal teeth on the front of the bucket cut through the rubble and earth, scooping them up into the bucket.

# EXCAVATOR

These mighty machines are seen on the largest building sites. They are used to dig the foundations beneath buildings, or to dig wide trenches. Their strong hydraulic arms (*see left*) are also used to pull down buildings, or they can be fitted with enormous claws to pick up heavy objects.

Beneath the driver's cab are two large Caterpillar tracks. These spread the weight of the excavator over a larger area and stop it from sinking into soft ground. The largest excavators can weigh 80 tons — that's as much as 25 fully grown elephants!

9

# There are many ways

## Going, going, gone

Not all buildings can be demolished cheaply and quickly by machines. Very tall buildings may need dynamite to knock them down. Sticks of dynamite are put in places in the building where they will have most effect. When they explode, they cause the building to collapse (*right*). It takes a lot of skill to demolish a building without damaging surrounding buildings and spreading rubble everywhere!

# to knock things down.

## Bulldozer

When a building has been knocked down, the rubble has to be cleared away. Machines called bulldozers (*below*) are fitted with huge blades at the front. They push the debris to one side where it can be loaded into trucks.

## Giant claw

The claw on the end of this machine (*right*) is used to pull down buildings. The driver's cab is fitted with bullet-proof glass to protect the operator.

# Machines are used to

## Tall cranes

The tallest cranes are put together in stages (*left*). They have long arms, or jibs, that sit on top of towers. Loads are lifted by cables and a hook from one end of the jib, while heavy weights on the other end stop the crane from falling over. This is called a tower crane.

## Eye in the sky

The crane driver sits in a small cab at the top of the crane (*right*). From here, he or she controls where the crane's arm is pointing and how much cable is run out to lift or lower the load.

# lift things into the air.

## Into the air

Once they have been set up, cranes are used to lift almost any object into place. It could be a section of pipe (*left*), metal girder, some glass for a window, or a load of concrete.

## Movable cranes

Not all cranes have to stay in one place. This mobile crane (*above* and *right*) is fitted onto a special truck. It has a long arm that can be extended and spun around.

# Machines have made

## Pick and shovel

Today, a single machine operated by one person can do the same work that used to take many people equipped with picks and shovels (*right*).

## Full steam ahead

Before powerful internal combustion engines and electric motors were invented, building machines were powered by other means. This shovel (*above*) was powered by a steam engine.

# building much easier.

## Trench digging

Endless bucket trenchers use a series of small buckets on a belt. As this belt moves around, the buckets scoop out the earth to dig a trench. Bucket trenchers, like this one from 1901 (*right*), were used for many years, long before the invention of hydraulic arms (*see* page 9).

## Steam press

Like the steam shovel (*see far left*), this roller (*left*) was powered by a steam engine. The roller's huge, heavy wheels were used to squash the surface of a road flat to make it smooth for vehicles to drive over.

### Rear engine

This scraper is fitted with two engines. The engine at the rear drives the rear wheels, pushing the scraper along.

### Collecting the load

This container can hold about 17 tons of earth — nearly the weight of 250 adults!

### The blade

The scraper's blade can be pushed up to 12 inches (30 cm) into the soil.

# SCRAPER

This machine is used to scrape up layers of earth, preparing the ground for a road. It has a huge blade underneath that digs up

## Hinged front
The tractor unit is linked to the rest of the scraper by a large hinge that bends to make turning easier.

## Tractor unit
The front of the scraper, which contains one engine and the driver's cab, is called the tractor unit.

## Powerful engines
In order to push and pull the scraper's blade through the ground, the engines need to be very powerful. Each engine of this scraper is as powerful as the engines from ten family cars!

the soil as the scraper drives forward. The soil is then collected in a huge container and carried to another site where the scraper can drop it. Sometimes, even the two engines in a scraper are not powerful enough and it may need to be pushed by another vehicle.

# A lot of machines are

## Digging it up

This backhoe loader has been fitted with a pneumatic drill (*left*). In this, air is squashed very hard, which forces a piston up and down. This piston smashes onto a tool, hammering it into the road.

## Fine grades

A grader is fitted with an angled blade. As the grader drives along, this blade pushes the soil to one side to create the flat, even surface. This is called grading. It can also be used to create even slopes (*below*).

# used to build a road.

## Squashing it flat

After the asphalt has been laid (*see* pages 20-21), a roller (*left*) is used to squash it flat and make it smooth. The heaviest roller can weigh 35 tons — that's the same as 12 elephants!

## Excavator

As well as demolishing buildings and digging trenches, excavators can be used to build roads (*left*). Their buckets can be used to move rubble and to grade soil to create an even surface.

**Exhaust**
As the engine burns fuel to work, it creates waste gases. These gases are carried out of the engine along a metal pipe called the exhaust.

**Controls**
On some road pavers, the steering wheel and other controls can be moved from one side of the paver to the other. This lets the driver keep a close eye on either side of the road.

**Hopper**
Dump trucks empty the hot asphalt into this large hopper at the front of the road paver.

**Conveyor belt**
This conveyor belt carries the asphalt from the hopper to the rear of the road paver.

### Hotplates

Once the asphalt has been spread over the road, special heated plates, called soleplates, flatten and smooth the asphalt out. Sometimes, these soleplates can be extended so the paver can lay a wider road.

# ROAD PAVER

Once a pathway has been dug for a road, the road's foundations are built by putting down layers of materials. The final layer is built by a road paver. This noisy, smelly machine moves forward slowly, spreading a thin layer of asphalt. This is a black, sticky substance that is mixed with stones. It can be squashed and shaped when it is hot and is rolled flat by a roller (*see* page 19) to make it smooth. When it cools, it sets hard enough to withstand heavy traffic. A paver is also used to replace old or damaged asphalt.

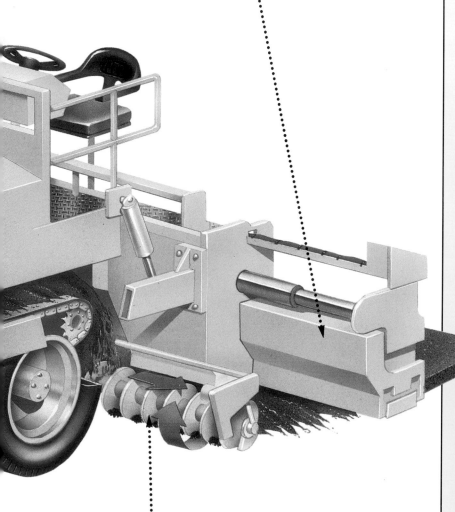

### Giant corkscrew

At the back of the road paver is a large screw called an auger. This auger spins slowly, spreading the asphalt evenly across the road.

# Massive machines

## Wheel and bucket

This enormous machine (*below*) is used in huge opencast mines. It is fitted with a massive wheel ringed with buckets. It is called a bucket-wheel excavator. The huge wheel at the front of the excavator spins around, and the buckets gouge out earth.

# are needed on mines.

## Life's a drag

This massive digging machine (*left*) is called a drag-line excavator. It throws out an enormous bucket on the end of a cable and then drags it back over the surface. As it is dragged back, sharp metal teeth on the front of the bucket scrape up the earth.

## Massive buckets

The buckets on a mining excavator need to be big (*right*). The largest buckets are wide enough to hold two family cars!

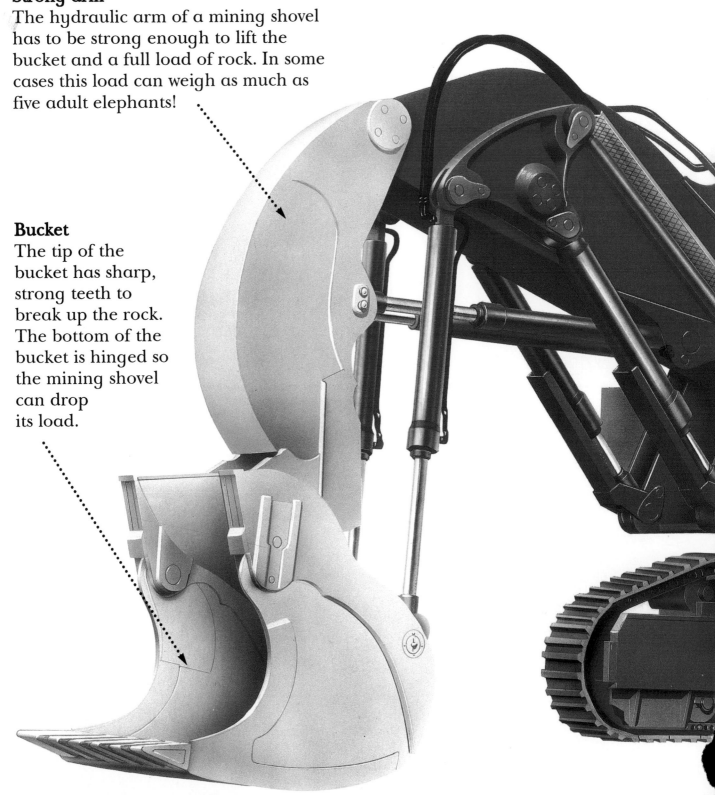

**Strong arm**
The hydraulic arm of a mining shovel has to be strong enough to lift the bucket and a full load of rock. In some cases this load can weigh as much as five adult elephants!

**Bucket**
The tip of the bucket has sharp, strong teeth to break up the rock. The bottom of the bucket is hinged so the mining shovel can drop its load.

# MINING SHOVEL

Not all mines are hidden deep beneath the ground. Sometimes, minerals lie close to or on the surface. To get at these minerals,

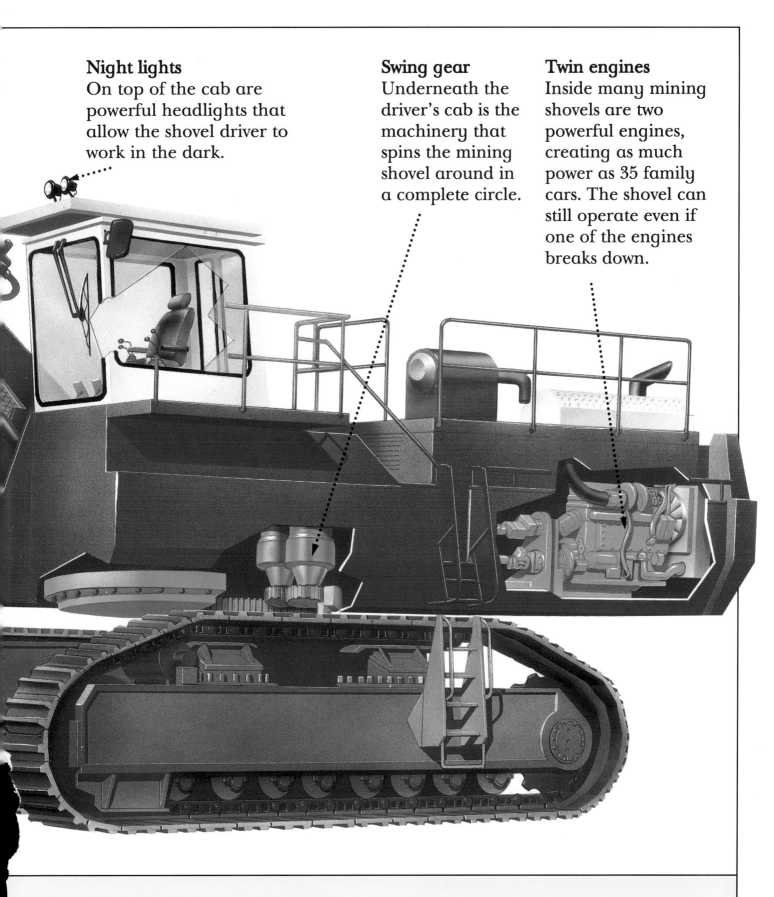

**Night lights**
On top of the cab are powerful headlights that allow the shovel driver to work in the dark.

**Swing gear**
Underneath the driver's cab is the machinery that spins the mining shovel around in a complete circle.

**Twin engines**
Inside many mining shovels are two powerful engines, creating as much power as 35 family cars. The shovel can still operate even if one of the engines breaks down.

huge machines (*see* pages 22-23) dig up the rock, creating enormous mines called opencast mines. One of these machines is a mining shovel. When it has filled its bucket, the driver can spin the shovel around and drop the load into a waiting truck.

# Machines are used to

## Long tunnel

The world's longest rail tunnel is the Seikan rail tunnel in Japan. It is 33.5 miles (54 km) long. It runs under the sea between the main island of Honshu and the island of Hokkaido. Here (*right*) you can see some of the machines used to dig the tunnel.

## Under the sea

The Channel Tunnel runs between England and France. Tunnel-boring machines (*see* pages 28-29) took over four years to dig the tunnel. This picture (*left*) shows the exciting moment when the two halves of the tunnel were linked.

# tunnel underground.

## Cutting coal

In an early underground coal mine, people had to dig the coal out with picks and shovels. Today, machines are used to cut coal from the coal face — the exposed coal on the walls of the mine (*above*).

## Exploding walls

This machine (*left*) is used to drill lots of little holes into a mine wall or coal face. The holes are loaded with explosives that are then set off. The wall shatters and falls to the floor. The rubble is gathered and removed.

### Cutting head
The cutting head is fitted with 100 cutting rollers and 200 picking teeth. These are made from a very tough metal called tungsten.

### Conveyor belt
This belt carries the rubble away from the tunnel face to waiting trucks.

### Drive motor
This huge electric motor spins the cutting head. The cutting head rotates about 1.5 to 3 times each minute.

### Push and pull
This motor makes sure that the cutting head is in the right position to cut the rock efficiently.

# TUNNEL-BORING MACHINE
Creeping forward at a speed of 5 inches (12 cm) a minute, these long machines are

### Fixing the segments
The segments lock together snugly and the joints are filled. In some cases, the tunnel may need to be watertight, so segments are bolted together and rubber seals used.

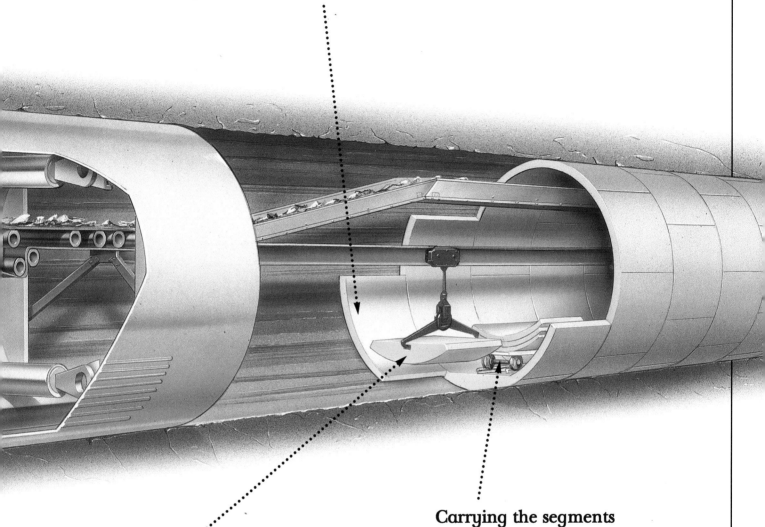

### Concrete and iron segments
The tunnel is lined with concrete and iron segments, each weighing up to eight tons!

### Carrying the segments
Each segment is lifted from its train car by a special crane. This crane then lifts the segments onto a special trolley that carries them along the tunnel.

used to dig tunnels. These tunnels can run under the seabed, through a mountain, or beneath busy city streets. At the front of a tunnel-boring machine (TBM), there is a huge cutting head that can rotate at different speeds to cut away the rock.

# Fantastic facts

• The largest mining excavator ever built is a dragline excavator called Big Muskie. It weighs 12,000 tons and has a bucket capacity of 37,000 gallons (168,000 liters)!

• The Italian inventor and artist Leonardo da Vinci designed the first rotating crane in 1480.

• The pneumatic drill was invented in 1861 by the French engineer Germain Sommeiller. It was first used to build the Mont Cenis Tunnel which runs under the Alps.

• The tallest mobile crane in the world is the Rosenkranz K10001. It weighs nearly 900 tons, but it can lift nearly 1,120 tons. Its arm can reach a height of 663 feet (202 m).

• Caterpillar tracks were invented in 1904 by American inventor Benjamin Holt. They were first used on a tractor in 1908.

• The tunnel-boring machines used to dig the Channel Tunnel were 49 feet (15 m) long and weighed 1,300 tons. Behind them were trains, each some 590 feet (180 m) long and with over 1,000 tons of equipment.

# Building words

## Backhoe
The extendable hydraulic arm at the rear of a backhoe loader. It digs by using an inward movement.

## Caterpillar tracks
These are wide belts that are fixed to a vehicle instead of wheels. They spread the weight of the vehicle over a large area and stop it from sinking into soft ground.

## Hydraulic
This refers to objects that are moved or powered by a liquid, such as water or oil. Hydraulic rams are used to move the arms in most diggers.

## Internal combustion engine
An engine where the burning of air and fuel occurs inside the engine's cylinders. Steam engines are not internal combustion engines because their fuel is burned outside the engine.

## Piston
A rod that fits inside a cylinder and is moved up and down by the pressure of a gas or a liquid.

## Pneumatic
This refers to objects that are moved or powered by compressed air, such as a pneumatic drill.

# Index

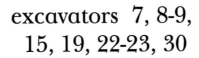

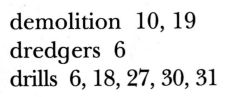
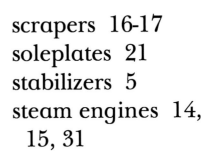
**PHOTO CREDITS**

Abbreviations: t-top, m-middle, b-bottom, r-right, l-left, c-center.
Pages 5, 9, & 19m — Charles de Vere. 6 & 18t — Roger Vlitos.
6-7, 11m, 12t, & 13 all — Liebherr UK Ltd. 7m — JCB. 7b,
11b, & 18b — Courtesy Finning UK Ltd. 10 all, 12b, 16,
19b, 23b, 26, 26-27, & 28 — Frank Spooner Pictures. 14
both & 15 — Mary Evans Picture Library. 21 — Blaw
Knox. 23t & 27t — Eye Ubiquitous. 24 — Eric
Blackadder. 27b — National Coal Board.